# THE
# BULL RING
## BIRMINGHAM

## PATRICK BAIRD

*including photographs by Anthony Spettigue*

SUTTON PUBLISHING

Sutton Publishing Limited
Phoenix Mill · Thrupp · Stroud
Gloucestershire · GL5 2BU

First published 2004

*Title page photograph:* The statue of Lord
Nelson overlooking St Martin's Church.
(*Anthony Spettigue*)
*Page 4:* The new Selfridge's building. (*Simon
Fletcher*)

**British Library Cataloguing in Publication Data**
A catalogue record for this book is available from the
British Library.

ISBN 0-7509-2920-0

Typeset in 10.5/13.5 Photina.
Typesetting and origination by
Sutton Publishing Limited.
Printed and bound in England by
J.H. Haynes & Co. Ltd, Sparkford.

Pride of place in the new £500 million Bullring development is this twice-lifesize statue of
a Hereford bull sculpted by Laurence Broderick. It stands 2.2m high, is 4.4m long and
weighs 6.5 tonnes. It was cast at the Pangolin Editions foundry in Chalford, Gloucestershire.
So popular has it become that miniatures of it are available to buy in St Martin's Church.
(*Simon Fletcher*)

# CONTENTS

# INTRODUCTION

Thursday 4 September 2003 saw the beginning of a new era in the history of the city of Birmingham with the official opening of the new Bull Ring, or Bullring, as the developers like to call it. The centre and heart of Brum has now returned to its original location.

To many people, even those who may never have visited Birmingham in their lives, the very name 'Bull Ring' is synonymous with the city. It is the traditional market centre with a long and unbroken history dating back to at least the twelfth century when the first market charter was granted to Peter de Bermingham in 1166 by King Henry II. This pre-dated charters granted to most other English towns, the thirteenth century being the period during which over 3,000 grants were given.

Twenty-three years later a second market charter was granted by Richard Cœur de Lion (Richard the Lionheart) to William, son of Peter de Bermingham, but this was merely a renewal or confirmation of the original charter. Richard was about to leave for the second crusade and needed to raise money for the expedition. In order to do this he travelled through the kingdom, confirming or calling in and granting new charters in return for suitable monetary remuneration. He was in Worcester on 12 November 1189 and from here he possibly came to Birmingham, where he signed an undated charter that also gave privileges to the monks of Bordesley (Worcestershire). This document was signed to William, son of Peter, who actually accompanied the King to the Holy Land, and was sealed at Canterbury on 2 December 1189.

Permission to hold a fair in his Manor of Birmingham for four days at Whitsuntide was granted to another William de Birmingham by Henry III in 1250. It is known that in 1309 the Lord of the Manor in Birmingham brought an action to defend his right to collect market dues, and he claimed that his predecessors had levied customary tolls before the Norman Conquest, but there is no evidence to corroborate this.

Birmingham's first historian, William Hutton, writing in 1781, informs us:

By the interest of Audomore de Valance, Earl of Pembroke, a licence was obtained from the Crown in 1319 to charge an additional toll upon every article sold in the market for three years towards paving the town. Every quarter of corn to pay one farthing, and other things in proportion. But, at the expiration of the term the total was found inadequate to the expense, and the work lay dormant for eighteen years, till 1337.

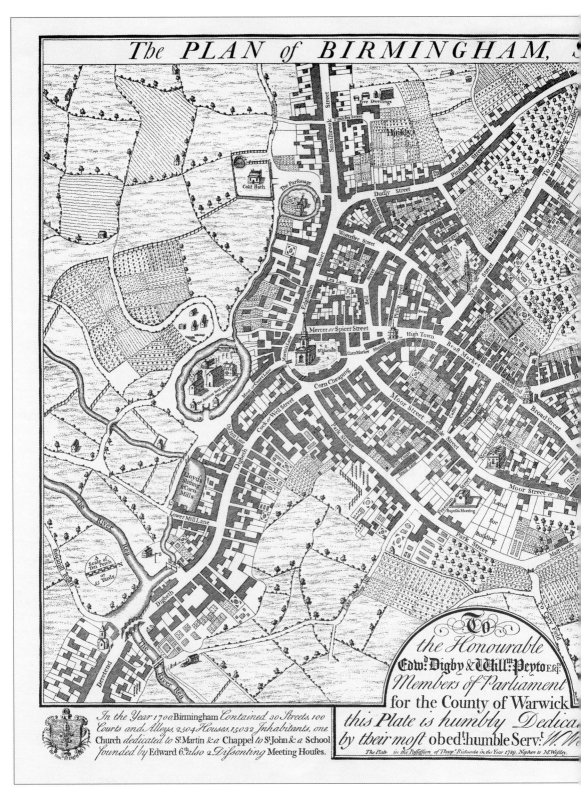

The PLAN of BIRMINGHAM,

In the Year 1700 Birmingham Contained 30 Streets, 100 Courts and Alleys, 2,504 Houses, 15,032 Inhabitants, one Church dedicated to St Martin & a Chappel to St John & a School founded by Edward 6th also 2 Dissonting Meeting Houses.

To the Honourable Edwd: Digby & Willm: Peyto Esqr: Members of Parliament for the County of Warwick this Plate is humbly Dedica by their most obedt humble Servt: W. W

The Plate is in the Possession of Theop Richards in the Year 1789, Nephew to Mr Westley.

'The Plan of Birmingham, Survey'd in the Year 1731' by William Westley. This is the first officially published map of Birmingham and on it Westley observes the following:

In the year 1700, Birmingham contained 30 Streets, 100 Courts and Alleys, 2504 Houses, 15032 Inhabitants, one Church dedicated to St Martin & a Chappel to St John & a School founded by Edward 6th, also 2 Dissenting Meeting Houses. The Increase of this Town from 1700 to Year 1731 is as follows: 25 Streets, 50 Courts and Alleys, 1215 Houses, 8254 Inhabitants, together with a new Church, Charity school, Market Cross, and 2 Meeting Houses.

*(Local Map Collection, Birmingham Central Library)*

These streets, thus dignified with a pavement, or rather their sides only, to accommodate the foot passenger, probably were High Street, the Bull Ring, Corn Cheaping, Digbeth, St Martin's Lane, Moat Lane, Edgbaston Street, Spiceal Street and part of Moor Street . . . The streets, no doubt, in which fairs were held, mark the boundaries of the town in the thirteenth century.

(William Hutton, *An History of Birmingham*, 1781; 4th edn, 1819, pp. 42–3)

A respected nineteenth-century Birmingham historian, Robert K. Dent, gives us a picturesque view of Birmingham in the fourteenth century by quoting another well-known figure, J.T. Bunce:

In the 14th century Birmingham was but a small place, a sort of county and town in union. The Church was probably somewhat above the centre of the town, standing on a green hill – sandstone rock below – sloping boldly from the brow at present occupied by High Street and New Street, to the actual site of the Church and thence falling somewhat abruptly to the present site of Smithfield, then occupied by the Manor House or dwelling of the Lords of Birmingham. Not far from the Church, at the end of what is now Edgbaston Street, stood the rectory house or parsonage, a clear stream running by it, forming, lower down, the moat of the Manor House, and thence passing on to fall into the Rea. There was probably a fringe of houses along the sides of the Bull Ring in the upper part in which stood the Old Cross . . . Digbeth constituted the road between Birmingham and Deritend, and was probably lined with houses built of timber framing, filled in with plaster, and having on the ground floor the open shops in which the smiths – then the chief artificers – had their hearths. It is possible, though not certain, that a few houses were dotted along Moor Street, and perhaps on the site of the narrow streets now running off from the opposite side of the Bull Ring. There would be houses in Spiceal Street, and perhaps one or two in St Martin's Lane; and these would be all.

(Robert K. Dent, *Old and New Birmingham*, 1880, p. 14)

For the next 200 years there are no surviving records relating to the growth of Birmingham, but then we get the first authentic contemporary account, given by John Leland, who made an itinerary of the whole country in the reign of Henry VIII. During 1538 he passed through the town, of which he says:

The beauty of Birmingham, a good market towne in the extreame parts of Warwikeshire, is one street going up alonge, almost from the left ripe [bank] of the brooke, up a meane hill, by the length of a quarter of a mile. I saw but one Parroch Church in the towne. There be many smiths in the towne that use to make knives and all mannour of cuttinge tooles, and many lorimers that make bittes, and a great many naylors.

The 'one street' was of course Digbeth, and the lower part of High Street, with a few narrow offshoots on either end, and a part of Spiceal Street on the western side of the church.

Birmingham never possessed a large market place, so as trade grew the market expanded into many of the streets in the centre of the town. By 1553 the Cornmarket, the Welsh Market and the English Market were all situated at separate places. Westley's map of 1731 shows the corn market in the Bull Ring, with the Shambles (a stretch of shops/buildings connected with various aspects of the butchery trade) above it and the beast market in the High Street, but not the Bull Ring. Thursday was the day on which the main cattle market was held, although a Monday cattle market, which was later discontinued, was opened in Deritend in 1776.

The year 1779 saw the passing of the first Improvement Act, and the regulation and reorganisation of the markets became the principal concerns of the Street Commissioners. It was the year when the cattle market was moved to Dale End.

In the early nineteenth century the Bull Ring was cleared and the general market moved there from the High Street in 1806. Eleven years on, Smithfield Market was opened on the site of the manor house moat; this absorbed the former markets for hay and straw as well as for cattle, horses, sheep and pigs. The year 1883 saw the wholesale vegetable market opened on part of the Smithfield site. By 1900 it had taken almost the entire area, although a weekly or bi-weekly second-hand market, known as the Rag Fair, was also held there from before 1912 until 1957.

East Prospect of Birmingham, 1732, drawn by William Westley. It shows St Martin's Church, and to its left the Manor House of the De Bermingham family and surrounding buildings bounded by the moat supplied by the River Rea – see foreground. To the right of St Martin's Church can be seen the Free School, founded by Edward VI, and to the right of that St Philip's Church, now Birmingham Cathedral. (*Prospect View Collection, Birmingham Central Library*)

The Street Commissioners had also opened a meat market in Jamaica Row, but this was superseded in 1897 by one situated in Bradford Street, to which slaughterhouses had been added.

The famous Market Hall was opened in 1835 as a general retail market but was gutted by an air raid during the Second World War, 105 years later. However, it continued as a market, with covered stalls being erected on the site until the early 1960s.

The origin of the name 'Bull Ring' is unclear. It is known that a tenement in 'le Bulryng' or 'le Bulringe' was sold in 1553. It is also unclear whether bull baiting actually took place here. William Hutton relates that a certain John Cowper, who lived in about 1530 at the Talbot in High Street, obtained from the Lord of the Manor three privileges, one being that he should whenever he pleased bait a bull in the Bull Ring (Hutton, *An History of Birmingham*, 2nd edn, 1783, pp. 57–8), but Joseph Hill, a later historian, says that these statements are merely traditional and inaccurate. Hutton also appears to contradict himself when he says 'the place which has obtained the modern name of Bull-ring, and which is used as a market for corn and herbs, was once an appropriation of the church . . .' (Hutton, *An History of Birmingham*, 2nd edn, p. 233).

The *Victoria County History of Warwickshire*, in a chapter on 'Sport, Ancient and Modern', states:

> that the amusement of bull-baiting was formerly very popular with the lower classes in Warwickshire. There are ample evidences; moreover there are men still living who remember the time when in Birmingham and elsewhere in the county, one of the leading features of the annual wake (which usually fell on the festival of the patron saint of the parish church) was the exhibition at the bull-ring. The last bull is said to have been baited in Birmingham in 1820, when the promoters were lodged in Warwick Gaol – a matter of surprise, seeing that the cruel practice was not legally inhibited until fifteen years later.
>
> (*Victoria History of the County of Warwickshire*, 1908, vol. 2, p. 416)

The last local reference to this cruel sport can be found in a letter written by A. Smith of Brierley Hill sent to the editor of *Aris's Birmingham Gazette* and dated 12 October 1835:

> SIR – It must be gratifying to every friend of humanity, that, during the last Session of Parliament, a bill, the provisions of which, if strictly enforced, will have the effect of abolishing the horrid and demoralising practice of Bull-baiting, was introduced and received the Royal assent. It therefore behoves the Ministers and Churchwardens of those parishes where the cruel system has been pursued, to avail themselves of the power now placed in their hands, and zealously to carry into effect the humane intentions of the framers and supporters of the bill, while

every sincere friend to humanity will cheerfully lend his assistance. As an individual deeply interested in promoting the happiness of the brute creation, I shall devote my time and labour in this good cause, and exert myself to render the bill effectual to the end designed. For want of such exertion, Bull-baiting was carried on to a horrible extent during the last wake at Brierley Hill, and thousands of people from distant parishes congregated together to enjoy this feast of blood. Three bulls were then baited on the Saturday evening previous to the wake Sabbath, and for four successive days they were torn and lacerated for their amusement in a manner too shocking to relate. Trusting that the diabolical sport will be speedily abolished, I remain, Sir, your obliged servant.

(Dent, *Old and New Birmingham*, pp. 486–7).

The Bull Ring has always been at the fore as a place where people, both resident and non-resident, could express their own views. The first of the Bull Ring 'spouters', and leader of a long line of orators, was the founder of Methodism, John Wesley. However, he met with a very mixed reception. In 1745 at one of his meetings a writer reports: 'stones and dirt were flying from every side almost without intermission for nearly an hour' and the bells of St Martin's were rung in an effort to drown his voice.

In 1766 it was the scene of a 'food' riot – one of several in the eighteenth century caused by spiralling prices. In September of that year rioters seized butter in the market priced at 10*d* and 'sold it at 7*d* and gave all the money to the dealers' (*Lloyd's Evening Post*, 10 September 1766). Later a labourer, thought to be a miner from Dudley, erected a 'standard' – an inverted mop – and called out 'redress of grievances', after which numbers of people went around forcing stallholders and grocers to sell bread, cheese, bacon and other provisions at a fixed price. A magistrate from Handsworth, John Wyrley Birch, eventually managed to restore order but not without the aid of eighty special constables armed with staves as well as the threat of military reinforcements. Another food riot occurred in 1782, when Black Country colliers invaded Birmingham via Wednesbury, where they forced a reduction in the cost of flour and malt. The colliers were soon joined by the nailers and spinners of the district. A peaceful group arrived in Birmingham at about 4.00 p.m. on 17 October and marched to the Bull Ring, where they negotiated with the 'officers of the town' a list of prices for malt, flour, butter, cheese and other goods before leaving. On 23 October a meeting of inhabitants ratified the price list, and also the appointment of 140 special constables to prevent further disorder. In addition a subscription was raised to subsidise the price of bread at a third of the normal retail price.

Perhaps the most well-known outbreak of violence occurring in the Bull Ring area was the Chartist Riot of 1839. A number of political gatherings at this time became so rowdy that shopkeepers and stallholders felt uneasy and appealed to the magistrates, who issued a warning against disorderly meetings and inflammatory speakers. Early in July a detachment of police from London, called in by the local

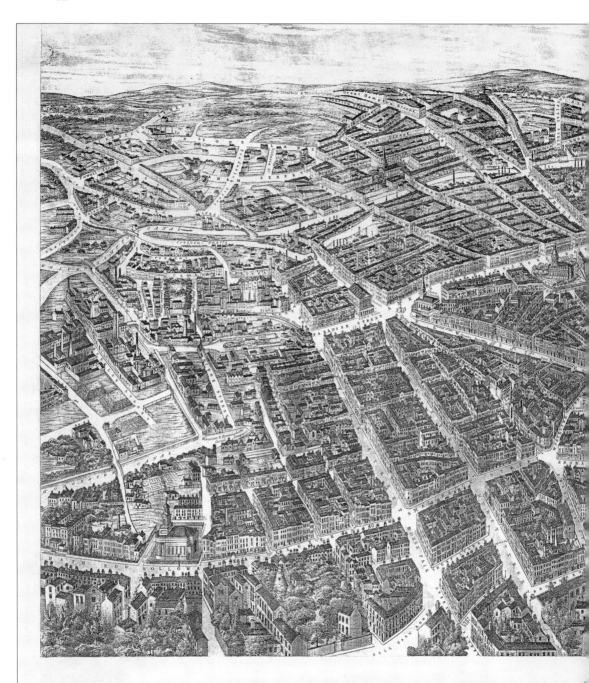

PANORAMIC VIEW

FROM A PLATE IN THE POSSESSION

OF BIRMINGHAM.

Ackerman's 'Panoramic View of Birmingham', 1847. The area around St Martin's Church shows the statue of Admiral Lord Nelson, with Digbeth and Deritend in the foreground, and High Street beyond. The plan also visibly shows how Birmingham has grown both residentially and industrially since the eighteenth century. (*Prospect View Collection, Birmingham Central Library*)

authorities, tried to break up a gathering in the Bull Ring. The area was cleared but the mob returned, and it was only through the intervention of the military that the police were not overpowered.

After a week or so the rioting began again in several parts of the town and became more serious. In the Bull Ring the rioters forced their way into several shops, breaking the windows of others as they went. Goods were seized, thrown into the street and kicked around the Bull Ring. A bonfire was started near Nelson's statue and fuelled with shutters from the shops. Some fifteen businesses were pillaged. Jewellery and plate were thrown about or stolen; paper, glass vessels, meat, tobacco and hardware all added to the chaos in the Bull Ring. Again police and troops were called out to restore order. Of the many people arrested, several were committed for trial at Warwick Assizes, with the result that four men and a boy were sentenced to death, later reduced to transportation.

For about the next 100 years the Bull Ring remained more or less the same – a spot well thought of, if not loved, by generations of 'Brummies' and visitors. On Thursdays and Saturdays the open street market, its stalls packed with garden produce, flowers and poultry, the hawkers with their barrows of fruit and vegetables, the kerbside vendors and the voices of fervent orators exhorting the crowds to buy their wares or to follow their religious or political beliefs all brought in throngs of people. Even after the Second World War, which brought havoc and chaos to part of the Bull Ring, Birmingham people found their way back to the area and soon business was booming yet again.

Great changes came about with the ultra-modern design of the John Laing-constructed Bull Ring Shopping Centre, opened by HRH The Duke of Edinburgh in 1964 to much admiration. Before 2000 this, however, was becoming dowdy and much neglected, so much so that something more suitable was desired. Thus at the end of the 1990s the entire area was demolished and a new phase began, eventually opening in September 2003 with the majority of visitors, and hopefully Brummies, liking what they saw. At long last the parish church was cleaned and the statue of Nelson replaced as close to its original position as possible.

Only time will tell if the much-written-about Selfridge's and the shopping centre will survive the ravages of the British weather and not descend into an ugly and dirty shadow of its former self, but what is true is that the Bull Ring will be at the heart of Birmingham life for many centuries to come, whether you spell it in its popular form 'Bull Ring' or in the advertising 'executive speak' as 'Bullring', copying the sixteenth-century 'Bulryng'.

*Patrick Baird, 2004*

# *Chapter One*

# *St Martin's Church*

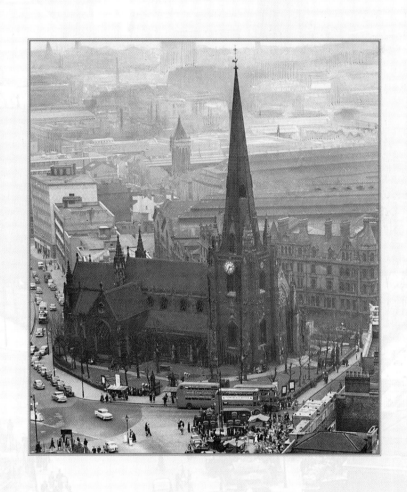

The effigy of an ecclesiastic in St Martin's Church. This print was published by J. Nicholls in 1842. (*St Martin's Box, Birmingham Central Library*)

*Below:* An impressive tomb in St Martin's Church. This photograph was taken by F. Crompton Lewis in September 1901. (*Warwickshire Photographic Survey, Birmingham Central Library*)

St Martin's Church from High Street. This print was drawn in 1824. The current view fron High Street to St Martin's is almost identical to this. (*St Martin's Box, Birmingham Central Library*)

St Martin's Church during the rebuilding of the spire. This work began on 31 May and was completed on 21 July 1853. (*St Martin's Box, Birmingham Central Library*)

The new spire completed. This print is thought to date from November 1855. In front can be seen the statue of Admiral Lord Nelson. (*St Martin's Box, Birmingham Central Library*)

*Left and opposite:* St Martin's underwent further reconstruction in 1872 when it was virtually rebuilt. These three photographs were taken at the time of this event. (*Large Views, Birmingham Central Library*)

The Bull Ring area and the church at the beginning of the Bull Ring's postwar reconstruction, 1959. (*St Martin's Box, Birmingham Central Library*)

*Opposite:* St Martin's photographed by Thomas Lewis in 1880 showing the completely rebuilt building. (*St Martin's Box, Birmingham Central Library*)

Flower arranging in St Martin's Church in 1975. (*St Martin's Box, Birmingham Central Library*)

# Chapter Two

# Around St Martin's: Digbeth & Deritend

*Above:* The 'Propper Chappell' of Deritend. Built in 1375, repaired in 1571 and demolished in 1737, it was replaced by the chapel (later 'church') of St John. (*Warwickshire Photographic Survey, Birmingham Central Library*)

Print of the chapel of St John, Deritend, by John Pickering, date unknown. (*Warwickshire Photographic Survey, Birmingham Central Library*)

The Golden Lion, High Street, Deritend, 1868. This half-timbered building stood almost opposite the Old Crown House and during the sixteenth century acted as a grammar school maintained by the Guild of St John the Baptist. Its most famous pupil was John Rogers, born in Deritend in 1500. His claim to fame was that he joined William Tyndale and Miles Coverdale in translating the Bible into English. In 1555 he was burned at the stake at Smithfield in London, becoming the first martyr during the reign of Queen Mary. The Golden Lion was removed from Deritend in 1911 and re-erected in Cannon Hill Park. (*Large Views, Birmingham Central Library*)

High Street in 1875, showing the Golden Lion to the left and the tower of the church of St John to the right. (*Large Views, Birmingham Central Library*)

*Opposite:* A print of High Street, Deritend, drawn by F. Mercer in 1876. (*Warwickshire Photographic Survey, Birmingham Central Library*)

Old Crown House, Deritend, from a print, *c.* 1850. This is the oldest inn in Birmingham. No one is sure of its exact date of erection, although it certainly dates from the fifteenth century – some say from about 1368. However, the first time it was mentioned by name was in 1589, when John Smalbroke of Yardley sold it to John Dyckson with John Hayberd as sitting tenant. The pub closed in the early 1990s but reopened in 1998 under the management of Oakcombe Ltd and its director, Patrick Brennan, following a £1.5 million refit. (*Warwickshire Photographic Survey, Birmingham Central Library*)

An early photograph of the Old Crown House, 1857. (*Warwickshire Photographic Survey, Birmingham Central Library*)

Digbeth looking towards the Bull Ring, 27 June 1902, a bank holiday celebrating the coronation of King Edward VII. Unfortunately, because of the king's illness, the coronation was postponed until 9 August of the same year. The photograph was taken by Percy Deakin. (*Warwickshire Photographic Survey, Birmingham Central Library*)

Pigs on High Street, Deritend, on the way to market, photographed by Thomas Clarke in September 1903. (*Warwickshire Photographic Survey, Birmingham Central Library*)

Jamaica Row, 1938. This was once the courtyard of the Black Boy Inn, which was probably named after Prince Charles, later Charles II, who was known as 'the black boy' because of his swarthy complexion. Jamaica Row disappeared beneath the 1960s redevelopment of the Bull Ring. (*Warwickshire Photographic Survey, Birmingham Central Library*)

Spiceal Street in the 1950s. The home of silk and linen merchants, this street has been known as Spiceal, Spicer or Mercer Street. In medieval times the shops here were occupied by the leading burghers of the town. (*Warwickshire Photographic Survey, Birmingham Central Library*)

Plenty of public transport, despite hold-ups: the junction of Digbeth and Rea Street in May 1934. (*Warwickshire Photographic Survey, Birmingham Central Library*)

*Opposite, top:* No improvements seemed to have been made in almost twenty years: traffic congestion at Rea Street and Smithfield Street, looking towards the city, in February 1952. (*Warwickshire Photographic Survey, Birmingham Central Library*)

*Opposite, bottom:* Continued traffic congestion along Smithfield Street in March 1953. The outline of Smithfield Market can be seen on the right-hand side of the road towards the left of the photograph. (*Warwickshire Photographic Survey, Birmingham Central Library*)

Even more problems at Digbeth near Rea Street in March 1953. (*Warwickshire Photographic Survey, Birmingham Central Library*)

Road-widening eventually took place at Digbeth during 1954 and 1955, the work being completed in July 1955. This photograph, taken in 1955, shows the improved road looking towards St Martin's Church and the Bull Ring. Digbeth police station can be seen clearly on the right. (*Warwickshire Photographic Survey, Birmingham Central Library*)

Traffic problems, however, continued in roads surrounding the Bull Ring, and this photograph, taken in June 1959, shows four lanes of parked vehicles and only one lane of moving vehicles in Edgbaston Street. (*Warwickshire Photographic Survey, Birmingham Central Library*)

This photograph from July 1959 shows the traffic in Jamaica Row. The vehicles parked on both sides of the street are causing delays, while a vehicle turning into Upper Dean Street is holding up the vehicles behind. Traffic emerging from Bradford Street is being delayed by traffic in Moat Row. (*Warwickshire Photographic Survey, Birmingham Central Library*)

# Chapter Three

# The Bull Ring until Postwar Reconstruction

A drawing of the Bull Ring by Samuel Lines, a well-known local artist, *c.* 1821. Lines was born at Allesley near Coventry in 1778, taught himself the rudiments of drawing and in 1794 was apprenticed to Mr Keeling, a clock-dial enameller and decorator from Birmingham, for whom he worked as designer. He was later employed by Henry Clay, the famous papier-mâché manufacturer, and also by the die-engravers Wyon and Halliday. His work included designs for decorating sword blades presented to officers who had distinguished themselves 'in some of our great victories over the French'. He helped in the foundation of the Birmingham School of Art in 1821, and on the formation of the Birmingham Society of Artists he was elected treasurer and curator, holding these offices until he was eighty years old. He died in 1863 aged eighty-five. On this print can be seen the 'ring' from which the Bull Ring is believed to have received its name from 'Bull Baiting which took place there' and the medieval butchers' shops known as 'The Shambles'. (*Birmingham Slide Collection, Birmingham Central Library*)

Another view of 'The Shambles' in the eighteenth century. (*Bull Ring Box, Birmingham Central Library*)

The Bull Ring from High Town, 300 years ago, showing the Market Cross, once used as a prison and classrooms for the Grammar School of King Edward VI before an actual school was constructed in New Street at the beginning of the eighteenth century. (*Bull Ring Box, Birmingham Central Library*)

More nineteenth-century prints of St Martin's and the Bull Ring. (*Bull Ring Box, Birmingham Central Library*)

The statue of Lord Nelson, 1891. To the left can be seen the entrance to the Market Hall, which was opened in 1835. Its interior was bombed in 1940, but the market remained open until 1963. The statue, the work of Richard Westmacott, had been unveiled on 25 October 1809 and was the first statue in Birmingham to be erected through public donations. Some Brummies believed it to be the first statue in the world to have been placed in honour of our great naval hero, but one had previously been unveiled in Montreal in 1808. (*Warwickshire Photographic Survey, Birmingham Central Library*)

The Bull Ring and St Martin's in 1890. Notice the advertisements high above ground level on the left of the photograph. (*Bull Ring Box, Birmingham Central Library*)

The Bull Ring Market, drawn by arguably Birmingham's greatest water-colourist, David Cox. Born within walking distance of the Bull Ring, in Heath Mill Lane, Cox lived from 1783 to 1859 and ended his days in a quiet Staffordshire village – Harborne – now a sought-after suburb of Birmingham. The work was painted after 1809, as the statue of Nelson can clearly be seen.
(*Bull Ring Box, Birmingham Central Library*)

Resting and drinking from the water fountain at the base of the Nelson statue. This photograph was taken by William Jerome Harrison in 1892. (*Bull Ring Box, Birmingham Central Library*)

Flowers bedeck the statue of Nelson on Trafalgar Day, 5 October 1897, photographed by Thomas Clarke. (*Bull Ring Box, Birmingham Central Library*)

Trafalgar Day, 1914. This was not long after the beginning of the First World War, so it was a very subdued celebration. (*Warwickshire Photographic Survey, Birmingham Central Library*)

A naval line-up on Trafalgar Day, 1953. (*Bull Ring Box, Birmingham Central Library*)

Kerb merchants in the Bull Ring selling cheap jewellery, toys and jumping jacks, photographed by Thomas Clarke, 1897. (*Bull Ring Box, Birmingham Central Library*)

Ice-cream sellers (probably Italian) in the High Street. Note the pillar-box on the right. This photograph was taken by Thomas Clarke in August 1897. (*Bull Ring Box, Birmingham Central Library*)

An open-air market photographed by Percy Deakin in May 1898. The vendor appears to be selling plucked chickens while a basket on the right contains live birds. The large arcaded building in the background was a fish market and the eighteenth- and nineteenth-century façades of the houses to the left sometimes concealed medieval timber-framed buildings. (*Bull Ring Box, Birmingham Central Library*)

The Bull Ring flower market, photographed by Percy Deakin in May 1898. This market, outside the Market Hall, was held on Tuesdays, Thursdays and Saturdays. (*Bull Ring Box, Birmingham Central Library*)

Many varied stalls were based inside the Market Hall, including an early Marks & Spencer, seen here. The exact date of the photograph is unknown, but it was probably taken sometime in the 1890s. (*Bull Ring Box, Birmingham Central Library*)

Stopping for a chat at the flower market, May 1900. (*Bull Ring Box, Birmingham Central Library*)

Ladies selling penny packets of lavender flowers, photographed by Percy Deakin in July 1901. (*Bull Ring Box, Birmingham Central Library*)

The Bull Ring in 1950. Many more shoppers are now milling around the market stalls and public transport appears to be abundant. (*Bull Ring Box, Birmingham Central Library*)

*Opposite, top:* Crowds in the Bull Ring in 1908. (*Bull Ring Box, Birmingham Central Library*)

*Opposite, bottom:* The Bull Ring in 1930, showing the influx of motor cars and vans. (*Bull Ring Box, Birmingham Central Library*)

Plants and flowers being sold in the market in 1950. (*Bull Ring Box, Birmingham Central Library*)

High Street at the junction with Phillips Street near the Market Hall, July 1952. (*Bull Ring Box, Birmingham Central Library*)

The Bull Ring to the right of St Martin's Church, July 1952. Note the well-known shops such as Woolworth's and Wheatlands furniture store. These and the others in the photograph were eventually demolished to make way for the ultra-modern 1960s Bull Ring Centre. (*Bull Ring Box, Birmingham Central Library*)

Shoppers wandering around the Bull Ring, 1952. (*Bull Ring Box, Birmingham Central Library*)

# Chapter Four

## *During & After Reconstruction*

A bird's-eye view of the Bull Ring construction, 1962.
(*Bull Ring Box, Birmingham Central Library*)

*Opposite, top:* Demolition of the old and the beginnings of the new, 21 May 1959.
(*Bull Ring Box, Birmingham Central Library*)

*Opposite, bottom:* Part of the new road system in place, with Woolworth's on the left and the Market Hall waiting to be demolished, July 1961. (*Bull Ring Box, Birmingham Central Library*)

The Bull Ring Centre beginning to take shape after the completion of St Martin's Circus, June 1962. (*Bull Ring Box, Birmingham Central Library*)

The Bull Ring Centre links across Smallbrook Queensway, September 1962. (*Bull Ring Box, Birmingham Central Library*)

Looking down towards where the open market stalls will eventually be situated, September 1962. (*Bull Ring Box, Birmingham Central Library*)

The Bull Ring Centre nearing completion, October 1963. (*Bull Ring Box, Birmingham Central Library*)

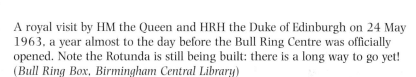

A royal visit by HM the Queen and HRH the Duke of Edinburgh on 24 May 1963, a year almost to the day before the Bull Ring Centre was officially opened. Note the Rotunda is still being built: there is a long way to go yet! (*Bull Ring Box, Birmingham Central Library*)

*Above:* The Queen on walkabout in the newly constructed outdoor market. (*Bull Ring Box, Birmingham Central Library*)

HRH Prince Philip, Duke of Edinburgh, after officially opening the Bull Ring Centre on 29 May 1964. To his left in the foreground is Alderman Frank Price, Lord Mayor of Birmingham. (*Bull Ring Box, Birmingham Central Library*)

Inside the Bull Ring Centre on opening day, 29 May 1964. (*Bull Ring Box, Birmingham Central Library*)

*Above:* The Bull Ring motif near the entrance to the indoor market in 1964. (*Bull Ring Box, Birmingham Central Library*)

Shoppers enjoying a well-earned rest in the area where the statue of Lord Nelson was moved to, giving them and him a panoramic view towards the markets, 1964. (*Bull Ring Box, Birmingham Central Library*)

The open-air market looking across to Lord Nelson, unseen but further to the right of the walkway, 31 July 1964. (*Bull Ring Box, Birmingham Central Library*)

The indoor market, looking towards the entrance to the bus station, August 1964. (*Bull Ring Box, Birmingham Central Library*)

Looking further into the indoor market, August 1964. (*Bull Ring Box, Birmingham Central Library*)

The tops of the market stalls, 30 July 1964. (*Bull Ring Box, Birmingham Central Library*)

Peering into the market stalls, 1965. (*Bull Ring Box, Birmingham Central Library*)

*Opposite:* The outdoor market and the recently completed Rotunda, December 1964. A landmark for miles around, the Rotunda was Grade II listed by English Heritage in August 2000. (*Warwickshire Photographic Survey, Birmingham Central Library*)

The Bull Ring Centre from Carrs Lane Church, 1965. (*Bull Ring Box, Birmingham Central Library*)

Looking across St Martin's Circus to the Rotunda, 1966. (*Bull Ring Box, Birmingham Central Library*)

A worker among the shoppers in the outdoor market close to St Martin's, 1966. (*Bull Ring Box, Birmingham Central Library*)

The outdoor market, the Centre and the 265ft-tall Rotunda, 1971. (*Bull Ring Box, Birmingham Central Library*)

The mall in the indoor market's Grand Parade, 1972. (*Bull Ring Box, Birmingham Central Library*)

A host of golden daffodils, 1972. (*Bull Ring Box, Birmingham Central Library*)

*Above:* Strolling in the Manzoni Gardens, 1972. The gardens were named after the designer of Birmingham's £35 million inner ring road scheme, Herbert John Baptista Manzoni, who lived from 1899 to 1972 and was City Engineer and Surveyor of Birmingham from 1935 to 1963. (*Bull Ring Box, Birmingham Central Library*)

Walking towards the main entrance of the indoor market near St Martin's Church, 1972. (*Bull Ring Box, Birmingham Central Library*)

A children's roundabout in the Bull Ring, 1972 – a clever way of preventing boredom during shopping with grown-ups! (*Bull Ring Box, Birmingham Central Library*)

A gentle stroll on a sunny day in the Bull Ring Centre, 1975. The Rotunda is prominent in the background. (*Bull Ring Box, Birmingham Central Library*)

*Below:* The illuminated Bull Ring at night in the 1970s. (*Bull Ring Box, Birmingham Central Library*)

# Chapter Five

# The Market Hall

Length 365 feet.

BIRMINGHAM

now erect

Mr CHARLES

The EXTERIOR of this BUILD

Printed & Published by William Daniell, at

MARKET HALL.

he Design of

, ARCHITECT.                                    Breadth 108 feet.

BEAUTIFUL BATH STONE.

aphic Establishment, 88, New Street, Birmingham.

A print of the Market Hall published during the time of its construction, 1828–35. (*Warwickshire Photographic Survey, Birmingham Central Library*)

The Market Hall from Worcester Street, 1840. Note the different types of cart and the general hustle and bustle. (*Warwickshire Photographic Survey, Birmingham Central Library*)

*Opposite:* The Market Hall west entrance at Worcester Street, photographed by George Whitehouse in 1901. The foundations of the Hall were laid in 1831 and by the beginning of 1835 the building was practically completed; although it should have opened on 8 January, the opening was postponed until 12 February. Accommodation was provided for 600 stalls fitted up for the sale of fruit, poultry, fish and fancy articles. (*Warwickshire Photographic Survey, Birmingham Central Library*)

The pet stalls and the fish stalls in the Market Hall in 1870. (*Warwickshire Photographic Survey, Birmingham Central Library*)

The central fountain in the Market Hall, 1870. This elaborate bronze fountain, surrounded by figures representing various manufactures and groups of flowers, fish and fruit, designed and erected by Messrs Messenger and Sons, was placed in the centre of the hall in 1851. The fountain, however, became an obstruction to trade and was removed to Highgate Park some thirty years later. (*Warwickshire Photographic Survey, Birmingham Central Library*)

*Above:* A general view of the interior of the Market Hall, photographed by Thomas Lewis in 1870. Lewis was a well-known local photographer who ran his business in Stratford Road, Sparkbrook, from the 1870s to at least 1914. (*Warwickshire Photographic Survey, Birmingham Central Library*)

The west entrance to the Market Hall at Worcester Street, photographed by A.G. Davis in 1895. (*Warwickshire Photographic Survey, Birmingham Central Library*)

The Market Hall, photographed by William Jerome Harrison in 1895. Harrison was born in Hemsworth, near Doncaster, in 1845, and qualified as a teacher, eventually moving to Birmingham from Leicester in 1880 together with his wife and ten children to become chief science master to the Birmingham School Board. His interest in photography began in 1881 when he purchased his first camera. The effects of industrialisation and urbanisation brought fears to some that the county of Warwickshire would change beyond recognition. This led Harrison to make a photographic record of the county for posterity, and so in 1884 he and other local photographers formed the Birmingham Photographic Society, which in turn led to the establishment of the Warwickshire Photographic Survey in 1890. Harrison died in 1908. (*Warwickshire Photographic Survey, Birmingham Central Library*)

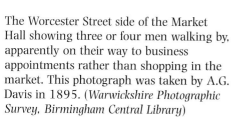

The Worcester Street side of the Market Hall showing three or four men walking by, apparently on their way to business appointments rather than shopping in the market. This photograph was taken by A.G. Davis in 1895. (*Warwickshire Photographic Survey, Birmingham Central Library*)

The east entrance to the Market Hall from the Bull Ring, 1901. The photographer was George Whitehouse, who took a sequence of photographs of the Market Hall for the Warwickshire Photographic Survey. More of these appear on pages 89–94. (*Warwickshire Photographic Survey, Birmingham Central Library*)

*Opposite, top:* The North Avenue of the Market Hall looking west, and showing fish stalls, 1901. (*Warwickshire Photographic Survey, Birmingham Central Library*)

*Opposite, bottom:* The view along the North Avenue looking east and showing fish and game stalls on the left and dining stalls on the right, 1901. (*Warwickshire Photographic Survey, Birmingham Central Library*)

A confectionery stall along the South Avenue, 1901. (*Warwickshire Photographic Survey, Birmingham Central Library*)

*Opposite, top:* Rabbits for sale along South Avenue, 1901. (*Warwickshire Photographic Survey, Birmingham Central Library*)

*Opposite, bottom:* A fish stall in the Market Hall, 1901. Note the prices of the fish. (*Warwickshire Photographic Survey, Birmingham Central Library*)

Bird fanciers' stall at the west end of the Market Hall, 1901. (*Warwickshire Photographic Survey, Birmingham Central Library*)

Something to make your mouth water! The oyster stall in the Market Hall, 1901. (*Warwickshire Photographic Survey, Birmingham Central Library*)

Flower stalls in the Market Hall, 1901. (*Warwickshire Photographic Survey, Birmingham Central Library*)

Customers being served at the Dining Hall, 1901. (*Warwickshire Photographic Survey, Birmingham Central Library*)

The Market Hall exterior from Bell Street, 1901. Bell Street was constructed by Thomas Kemsey in 1715, on land leased by William Bell of Alvechurch, and it linked Spiceal and Worcester streets. It disappeared during the reconstruction of the Bull Ring in the 1960s. (*Warwickshire Photographic Survey, Birmingham Central Library*)

The North Side of the Market Hall with a view of Phillips Street, 1901. Phillips Street was named after William Phillips, to whom the land originally belonged. His family also gave land for the building of St Philip's Church in Colmore Row (now Birmingham Cathedral). (*Warwickshire Photographic Survey, Birmingham Central Library*)

Workers stop to pose for the photographer on Bell Street, 1910. (*Warwickshire Photographic Survey, Birmingham Central Library*)

The Market Hall clock, photographed on 8 October 1935. The clock was not as old as certain continental clocks constructed on a similar principle, but it was a very ingenious mechanism, and children (and even adults) visiting the Market Hall generally made a point of being within sight of the clock as the hour hand approached its appointed spot on the dial and the figures prepared to strike the bells.

It was not originally in the Market Hall at all but in the Imperial Arcade, Dale End, where it was placed in about 1883. It ceased to function for some twenty years and was removed to the Market Hall. The mechanism was renovated, the bells recast, and in 1936 it was re-erected on a veranda over the Market Superintendent's office. There were four figures on it, three knights and an elaborately costumed lady, who struck the bells. The largest bell weighed 3cwt, the two middle figures were each 7ft 6ins high, the outer ones 6ft and they were made of solid oak. The dial of the clock was 5ft across and the pendulum weighed 2cwt.

Unfortunately, in September 1940, the Market Hall fell victim to a bombing raid and the clock was destroyed. (*Warwickshire Photographic Survey, Birmingham Central Library*)

A scene of devastation
on the morning after the
air raid, 9 September
1940. (*Warwickshire
Photographic Survey,
Birmingham Central
Library*)

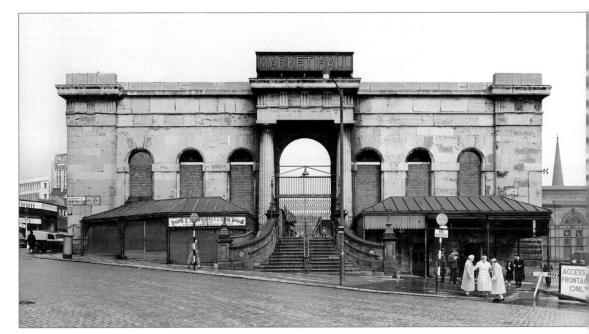

The Worcester Street entrance to the Market Hall in the 1950s. Although the hall had been gutted by an incendiary bomb, the shell continued to be used as a market until redevelopment swept it away. (*Warwickshire Photographic Survey, Birmingham Central Library*)

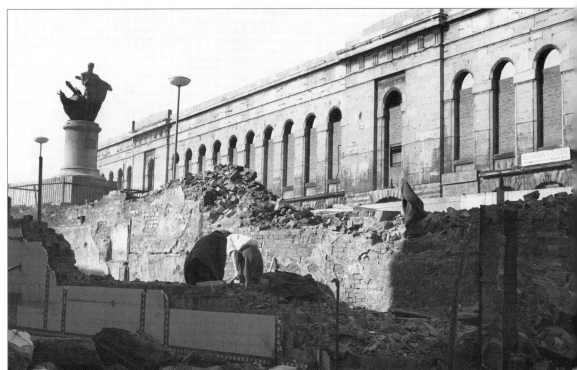

The Market Hall from the Bull Ring by the statue of Lord Nelson, 1960. The outer walls were eventually demolished in 1963. (*Warwickshire Photographic Survey, Birmingham Central Library*)

# Chapter Six

# Countdown to Demolition

People walking through the market, as seen from the Rotunda, July 1999. (*Anthony Spettigue*)

The Rotunda, St Martin's Circus, Queensway, and the Manzoni Gardens in the foreground to the right behind the coach – a view destined not to last much longer, June 1999. (*Anthony Spettigue*)

*Opposite:* St Martin's Church and the open fruit and vegetable market from the Rotunda, July 1999. (*Anthony Spettigue*)

Manzoni Gardens, Bull Ring, looking towards Smallbrook, Queensway, July 1999. The gardens had disappeared under a bulldozer by the end of 2000. (*Anthony Spettigue*)

The Bull Ring Centre and Smallbrook, Queensway, from the top of the Rotunda, July 1999. (*Anthony Spettigue*)

An increasing eyesore: the Kingsway furniture store, formerly the Woolworth building, in the Bull Ring, advertising its final offers before closing down. (*Anthony Spettigue*)

An unknown couple who just wanted to pose for the camera for posterity, in the Bull Ring area near Moor Street, July 1999. (*Anthony Spettigue*)

Another unattractive part of the Bull Ring area showing one of its many subways with St Martin's House ahead, July 1999.
(*Anthony Spettigue*)

The sign – Bull Ring 5 – denoting the old postcode and fixed to the railings of St Martin's Church, July 1999.
(*Anthony Spettigue*)

St Martin's House Parade looking empty and forlorn. Not long before this photograph was taken in July 1999 four sales kiosks stood close by. (*Anthony Spettigue*)

Edgbaston Street close to the rear entrance of the Midland Red bus station, July 1999. (*Anthony Spettigue*)

At the corner of Gloucester and Edgbaston streets, July 1999. The former S&U Stores building stood on this site from the late 1950s until its demolition in 1999. (*Anthony Spettigue*)

The Rag Market in Edgbaston Street, July 1999. It closed on 8 January 2000 and the traders moved to a temporary home in the Midland Red bus station in Station Street. The bulldozers moved in during the following week to make way for a new market hall. The Rag Market was opened in the mid-1950s to house stall holders from the old Jamaica Row market, itself a victim of modernisation in the 1960s. (*Anthony Spettigue*)

Despite the knowledge that the area would be disrupted in the not-too-distant future, the outdoor market remained busy. This photograph was taken looking towards New Street/High Street in July 1999. (*Anthony Spettigue*)

Another view of the Bull Ring open market, this time looking towards Moor Street, Queensway, July 1999.
(*Anthony Spettigue*)

Flower sellers under the arches of St Martin's Circus, Queensway, close to the Mark One clothes store in August 1999.
(*Anthony Spettigue*)

An interior view of Birmingham Wholesale Fruit and Vegetable Market in Pershore Street. This photograph was taken at 7 o'clock one morning in August 1999.
(*Anthony Spettigue*)

A view of the Bull Ring Centre from the road on a quiet, traffic-free morning in July 1999. (*Anthony Spettigue*)

A densely built-up area approached by subways, sandwiched between St Martin's Circus, Queensway, July 1999. (*Anthony Spettigue*)

A derelict Moor Street railway station in July 1999. Moor Street is one of Birmingham's oldest streets. It was originally called 'Mole Street', a corruption of *moladum* – a mill. It is known that there was a watermill here until the end of the seventeenth century. On Westley's plan of Birmingham of 1731 the roadway is shown as 'Moor Street or Mole Street'. (*Anthony Spettigue*)

Moor Street railway station sidings, with the 1960s Bull Ring Centre in the background, July 1999. (*Anthony Spettigue*)

The gates to the derelict Moor Street railway station in July 1999. (*Anthony Spettigue*)

Moor Street, Queensway, showing the railway station in the centre and St Michael's Roman Catholic Church to the right, July 1999. (*Anthony Spettigue*)

St Martin's House on the left and St Martin's Church on the right, photographed from the top of the Rotunda, July 1999. (*Anthony Spettigue*)

# Chapter Seven

# Towards Reconstruction

The Bull Ring Shopping Centre closed on 26 June 2000, but the outdoor market remained. This picture shows Bill Short, photographed in July 2000. He lived in Stephenson Tower over New Street station for many years and often hired the shopmobility vehicle to get around the markets. He was well known by the market stall holders and when he died in July 2001 they collected funds and had a wreath made in the shape of a chair – presumably a wheelchair.

Bill was one of six children and was brought up in the Kingstanding area of the city. He had been in the Sherwood Foresters and had retired at the age of fifty-five from British Leyland twenty years before this photograph was taken. His dog, photographed with him, although possessing a sharp bark did not have any teeth! (*Anthony Spettigue*)

A temporary footpath from Edgbaston Street and St Martin's Church viewed from below St Martin's Circus, Queensway, November 2000. (*Anthony Spettigue*)

The former site of Manzoni Gardens, St Martin's Circus, Queensway, November 2000. It has now gone forever. (*Anthony Spettigue*)

The end of Kingsway furniture store at the side of St Martin's Circus, Queensway, November 2000 (*Anthony Spettigue*)

The demolition of the multi-storey car park near Edgbaston Street, which had been disused for many years The foreground shows St Martin's Church car park in November 2000. (*Anthony Spettigue*)

A new road layout at the site of Selfridge's store. Moor Street railway station is on the right. (*Anthony Spettigue*)

Edgbaston Street: construction of the new Rag Market is shown on the left. The new food/fish market, opened in September 2000, is in the centre of the photograph. (*Anthony Spettigue*)

A temporary walkway leading to New Street from Edgbaston Street, March 2001. (*Anthony Spettigue*)

A temporary walkway leading to Edgbaston Street from the Rotunda, showing the indoor food/fish hall and the newly constructed Rag Market, March 2001. (*Anthony Spettigue*)

The final phase of the demolition of the 1960s Bull Ring Centre, Edgbaston Street, March 2001. (*Anthony Spettigue*)

Cranes dominate the skyline as viewed from a temporary walkway, as shown across the centre of the photograph, June 2001. (*Anthony Spettigue*)

*Opposite, top:* The site of the new Selfridge's store, April 2001. Moor Street railway station is on the left. (*Anthony Spettigue*)

*Opposite, bottom:* The site of the new shopping malls and Selfridge's store (top right), June 2001. (*Anthony Spettigue*)

The site of the new Debenham's store, at the corner of Edgbaston Street and Smallbrook, Queensway, viewed from the fifteenth floor of the Rotunda, June 2001. (*Anthony Spettigue*)

The site of Selfridge's store seen from the Rotunda. Moor Street railway station is on the left. (*Anthony Spettigue*)

At the rear of St Martin's Church, Selfridge's can be seen taking shape – at this time looking like the work of the Barcelona architect Antoni Gaudi, September 2001. (*Anthony Spettigue*)

A panoramic view of the construction of the new centre showing foundations and the beginning of the shops to the left of St Martin's Church, summer 2001. (*Mary Rose Salmon*)

Selfridges in December 2001. (*Anthony Spettigue*)

St Martin's Church from High Street, December 2001. (*Anthony Spettigue*)

The construction of the Bull Ring shopping malls from New Street, March 2002. (*Anthony Spettigue*)

Debenham's store at the junction of Smallbrook Queensway and Edgbaston Street taking further shape, March 2002. (*Anthony Spettigue*)

The Bull Ring development at the junction of High Street and New Street. The Rotunda is to the right, March 2002.
(*Anthony Spettigue*)

Selfridge's (right) is well under way. St Martin's is being cleaned. The famous shape of the Rotunda is in the centre, September 2002.
(*Anthony Spettigue*)

A large item being delivered to the Bull Ring development site on a Sunday morning. It was photographed in Moat Lane while everywhere was quiet, November 2002. (*Anthony Spettigue*)

The development is now becoming recognisable, particularly with Selfridge's on the right, December 2002. (*Anthony Spettigue*)

The outdoor market and the continuing cleaning of St Martin's Church, February 2003. (*Anthony Spettigue*)

The almost-complete Bull Ring with the now dominant shape of Selfridge's, February 2003. (*Anthony Spettigue*)

The new outdoor market with the Rotunda and the partly cleaned St Martin's Church in the background, April 2003. (*Anthony Spettigue*)

An impressive view of the spire of St Martin's Church during refurbishment with the Rotunda behind, April 2003. (*Anthony Spettigue*)

The irregular shape of Selfridge's overshadowing St Martin's Church, April 2003. (*Anthony Spettigue*)

Moor Street railway station during continuing refurbishment, April 2003. (*Anthony Spettigue*)

A walkway close to the Rotunda – part of the former St Martin's Circus, Queensway. Debenham's store is in the centre and New Street railway station is on the right, August 2003. (*Anthony Spettigue*)

A new car park erected opposite Selfridge's store, photographed in June 2003. Note the futuristic footbridge which links the two buildings. (*Anthony Spettigue*)

Moor Street, Queensway, area with the Bull Ring in the background, July 2003. (*Anthony Spettigue*)

Edgbaston Street, with the new Debenham's store on the left and the indoor food hall on the right, July 2003. (*Anthony Spettigue*)

Bull Ring construction workers enjoying a lunchtime break in Edgbaston Street, July 2003. (*Anthony Spettigue*)

The new Bull Ring and the recently refurbished St Martin's Church, photographed from Edgbaston Street, July 2003. (*Anthony Spettigue*)

# Chapter Eight

# Opening Day

The statue of Lord Nelson at long last in its rightful place. In the 1960s redevelopment the statue was moved to an out-of-the-way site opposite Moor Street station, on the roof above a public toilet. For years it was hoped that it would be moved to an appropriate location and the new scheme now finds it as close as possible to the original position overlooking St Martin's Church. (*Anthony Spettigue*)

*Below:* Thursday 4 September 2003 saw the opening of the new shopping and pedestrianised centre, referred to by the developers as 'The Bullring', amid great publicity, and apprehension among some Birmingham citizens. Here is the entrance to the centre at the junction of New Street and High Street on opening day. (*Anthony Spettigue*)

Crowds celebrating the opening at St Martin's Walk. (*Anthony Spettigue*)

Waiting to be let into the centre at Rotunda Square. The base of the Rotunda can be seen on the right. (*Anthony Spettigue*)

St Martin's Square from the left side of St Martin's Church in the early evening. The gap between the two sets of shops is the walkway to New Street and High Street. (*Anthony Spettigue*)

A view of part of the centre from St Martin's Square. Borders bookshop is on the left. (*Anthony Spettigue*)

An interior view of the shopping centre. Notice the glass roof from which most of the lighting comes. (*Anthony Spettigue*)

The juxtaposition of old and new, contrasting St Martin's Church with two pieces of modern architecture, with particular attention drawn to the imaginative Selfridge's store immediately to the left of St Martin's. This building has been the subject of much controversy since the inception of the scheme, with most people being sceptical about its design and location next to the much-loved parish church. Yet since opening day this has proved to be a winner. Not everyone likes it, but many more now think it to be a stunning creation, despite its lack of windows and its 15,000 non-corrosive aluminium discs. (*Anthony Spettigue*)

Inside the centre showing two of the entrances to Selfridges. (*Anthony Spettigue*)

The surreal footbridge now completed, leading from Selfridges to a car park opposite. (*Anthony Spettigue*)

Looking down from the footbridge to Moor Street car park, with a steam locomotive at Moor Street station. Everything looks like models rather than the real thing. (*Anthony Spettigue*)

The revamped Moor Street railway station from the Bullring Shopping Mall. (*Anthony Spettigue*)

A general view showing some of the many people on opening day hoping for a good look around. (*Anthony Spettigue*)

A view from the terrace outside the front entrance of Selfridges, looking towards St Martin's Church. (*Anthony Spettigue*)

A view of the terrace outside Selfridge's showing St Martin's Church on the left and part of the new development in the centre. Selfridge's is the most astonishing building in Birmingham today. Costing £40 million and designed by Future Systems, architects of the Space Age style press pavilion at Lord's Cricket Ground, it is based on a chain-mail dress designed by Paco Rabanne. During opening day, 4 September 2003, 94,000 people visited the store and within a month this had increased to 1.3 million. So successful has the shop been that the company is now investing hundreds of thousands of pounds in an expansion programme. Over 270,000 people visited the Bullring on its first day of opening, and within two weeks this had risen to 2 million – thus proving that interest in the new development is substantial. (*Anthony Spettigue*)

# ACKNOWLEDGEMENTS

**M**y grateful thanks are due to Birmingham Central Library Local Studies and History Service, Mary Rose Salmon and above all Anthony Spettigue, who has kept a continuing photographic record of the Bull Ring since the decision was made to demolish it and rebuild. His enthusiasm and pride for the City of Birmingham as a whole have never left him.

The photographs and illustrations from Birmingham Central Library are housed with the Local Studies and History Service. The Warwickshire Photographic Survey, to which most of the non-current photographs in this book belong, is a collection of some 25,000 images taken at intervals between 1889 and the late 1940s. This forms a small part of numerous photographic collections available at Birmingham Central Library, which also include 22,000 or so local, national and international photographs taken by the late nineteenth- and early twentieth-century Birmingham photographer Sir John Benjamin Stone and topographical images taken by Francis Frith and Francis Bedford. The library prides itself on having what is probably the largest collection of visual materials available in any public library in the United Kingdom and is always happy to accept donations of old or current photographs of the Birmingham area.

A view of the centre looking towards Debenham's. (*Anthony Spettigue*)